FROM GREEN TO GOLD

OTHER BOOKS BY
HAROLD ENRICO

Now, A Thousand Years From Now
Sono Nis Press, 1975

Rip Current
Sono Nis Press, 1986

Dog Star
Cacanadadada Press Ltd., 1990

A Second Earth
Ronsdale Press, 1997

From Green to Gold

New & Selected Poems

Harold Enrico

RONSDALE PRESS

FROM GREEN TO GOLD

RONSDALE PRESS
3350 West 21st Avenue
Vancouver, B.C., Canada V6S 1G7
www.ronsdalepress.com

Typesetting: Julie Cochrane, in New Baskerville 11 pt on 13.5
Cover Design: Brendan Beardsley
Paper: Ancient Forest Friendly Silva — 100% post-consumer waste, totally
    chlorine-free and acid-free

Ronsdale Press wishes to thank the following for their support of its publishing program: the Canada Council for the Arts, the Government of Canada through the Book Publishing Industry Development Program (BPIDP), and the Province of British Columbia through the British Columbia Publishing Tax Credit Program and the British Columbia Arts Council.

Library and Archives Canada Cataloguing in Publication

Enrico, Harold, 1921–
    From green to gold: new & selected poems/Harold Enrico.

ISBN 978-1-55380-067-5

    1. Northwest, Pacific — Poetry. I. Title.

PS3555.N74F76 2009   811'.54   C2008-904554-8

At Ronsdale Press we are committed to protecting the environment. To this end we are working with Markets Initiative (www.oldgrowthfree.com) and printers to phase out our use of paper produced from ancient forests. This book is one step towards that goal.

Printed in Canada by Marquis Book Printing, Quebec, Canada

CONTENTS

New Poems

from Dog Star

—

from A Second Earth

ACKNOWLEDGEMENTS

Publication of this book was made possible by John Enrico's sharp editing eye and fine ear, Brendan Beardsley's inspired artistic hand, Lea Enrico Beardsley's comprehensive direction, and the expert guidance of Ronald Hatch of Ronsdale Press.

"Madam" first appeared in *Prism International* in 1970; "I Hold a Beast, An Angel, and a Madman in Me" appeared in *Botteghe Oscure* and in the anthology *A Garland for Dylan Thomas* (ed. George J. Firmage).

The title "I Hold a Beast, An Angel, and a Madman in Me" is an excerpt from a Dylan Thomas letter. The title "And Love, Love Sang Toward" is a line in Theodore Roethke's poem, "The Shape of the Fire." The poem titled "Le Système Nerveux" is named in recognition of Paul Valéry's description of poets.

New Poems

And Love, Love Sang Toward

I

Summer was all light over the water,
flooding the rock, chasing the lizard,
caressing the leaf, warming the worm,
driving the mole deeper into the ground.

Summer was all air, clear of clouds,
pushing the darkness away from the stone,
crying in the skin of the frog,
crawling with the crayfish.

Summer was the light crowning my father's head,
as waist-deep in the dazzling water,
he cast line and fly over the riffles
drowned by the ouzel's cries.

Summer was the day over the river,
the sun shining on my father's hands,
a gleaming bracelet around his wrist,
offering the river all his love.

II

Fields are all birds in the morning.
Trees become light.
Mist drifts away with the river.
A stone laps water and air.
Someone walks on the water,
talks with the kingfisher's voice in the reeds.

The sun carries the morning into noon.
A grasshopper's wings brush my cheek.
Now shall I go forward?
My father striding the golden water,
offers me his arm.
Carry me, lucky feet, safely over slippery stones.
Father, guide my ankle bones.
Now shall I go forward in the light of my skin
deep in the night of the water?

A minnow brushes my thigh.
The river is ice in my ears.
Hear, what did the otter say?
My father is a darkness,
my mother a shadow over a root.

Pull me to the edge of the water,
Father, now I rise from the night.
Sway, light, over the archway of trees.
Sway, star.
Father, I love you.

III

I wait for my father in the night.
Stayed under the arc light playing games
until I hear his footsteps on the stones.

My grandmother's house smelled of apples.
She kept them all winter under her bed.
Boy! Boy! Get down from that tree!
Somewhere a bird sang Willow-Willow-Wide.
I caught a goldfinch and put it in a box.
I heard it dying, its head under its wing.
There was a moon in the wind
and a wind on the moon.

In the morning sheep grazed upon the hill.
I heard them bleating in my sleep.
The valley smelled green and sharp.
I came to a river, the shapes of trees
on the far bank: aspens, poplars swaying in the air.

Morning moved coolly across the water.

IV

Nè dolcezza del figlio, nè la pieta
*del vecchio padre . . .**

Talk to me, tendrils of time,
of the trials of voyage
in the dark speech of the father:

Figlio! Figlio! Figlio!

Night moves through night past the open window,
morning toward morning around the house.
My father walks through the blackbirds' voices,
drops to the edge of the stream.

What did the snake say to the grassblade?
The worm to the apple?
The sun to the tree?

Light opens the clouds.
There is light on the leaf
but night's in the stone.
A cold wind kisses my wrist.

My mother's shadow says to the rose "Be still."
The shadow of the rose says "Be still."
What did the rose say to me?

Now shall I go forward?
Mother, Mother, my bones are cold.

V

I cry to the hawk, now dust and bone,
in the earth between root and stone
to rise into the sky and soar
where he had soared over father and son,
in the light of a long-ago Eden.

* Dante's *Inferno*, Canto xxvi: Ulysses ("Nor fondness for my son, nor
reverence for my old father . . .")

Summer Interlude

The morning lies a lake of light
between hemlock hills and fields of hay,
while barns shine red as apples, houses, white
and gold as bread. Lilac branches sway
over fences along orchard roads
where dust will whirl away with August thunder.

Let robins guzzle cherry plunder
and blackbirds whistle in the thorns! Loads
of hay shuffle uphill like bears.
The ram beside the creekbed shakes his bell.

In seven fields black cattle graze with mares.
An old man dozes by a grassy well.
Deep meadows overflow the oval day
like rivers. Up the well-yard stile, whose daughter
steps high with Mason jars of icy water
for three dark men mowing the silver hay?

Voices

Walking beneath the trees the first day of June,
we stop and listen to a speckle-breasted thrush
pour out his song from limb to limb, full-throated, strong,
the notes cascading, phrase after phrase,
like molten silver from the alder leaves,
until we draw too near and spook him so he flies away.

It is as if all winter we have been living in a foreign town,
listening to a language we do not understand
when on a crowded bus a young woman's contralto voice
soars above the murmur of foreign voices,
singing out in English: "I love you! *I love you!*" over and over.

And we are suddenly back home.

My Father's House

Light moves, lifts the lake and trees. A stone
falls from a cliff. A mole's brown skeleton
lies in the sand. A bee drones in a flower.
I bite into an apple, summer-green and sour.
The pine-peaked towns, the clover meadows leap
the lake shore. The cloudy mountains creep
as slow as glaciers. My father's fingers tie
line to leader and Thunder-and-Lightning fly.
Trout dip around a yellow shoal. Across
the lake in Saxony, my father's house,
its blue-tiled roof, the castle clock,
shine in the sun. Upon a rock
I write my brother's name, the easy sleeper.
"Lord, why hast Thou made me my brother's keeper?"

The Ark

Our house, ark-roofed, careens across the flood
of autumn light, buffeted by golden auroras.
Gone wild, it whirls through maelstroms of fallen leaves,
scrapes reefs of shade, tempts shipwreck
on bright shoals of dahlias, flaming weeds.
Abandoned to the light that drowns the earth,
the pitiless deluge rained down by the sun,
we ride the flood all day.
Steer safely through deep grasses, roots and rocks,
hurtle toward shores the night had coveted
with nothing to save but ourselves in love.
And then the flood recedes,
our keel grinds aground and we almost flip over,
but right again in the failing light, the falling dark.
The moon, dove-breasted, sails the sky,
holding an olive branch in her beak in the name of love.

Sea Music

These were the acres of my father's dominion:
his island's sea, his blue-green waters,
his drowning forests sighing to the sea-wind's music.

These were the faces of my mother's mountains,
peaceful valleys, waves hurled at the moon,
forests sighing to the sea-wind's music.

And these were the gardens of my mother's daughters,
far from the voices of my father's lovers,
children laughing under the salty leaves,

the crickets they carried in willow cages
singing them the echoes of my father's sea-songs.

A Book of Birds

The meadowlark sings out
all the names of morning,
the purest vowels
beginning the day's declension,
paradigm after paradigm,
chimed in easy inflections,
over and over on the fence post
by the highway,
noun after noun for the verb of the sun —
light in the present tense,
recreating the world.
In the beginning was
its imperative verb.

But listen: more voices
compose a book of birds:
the phoebe's two-word vocabulary,
the thrush's alphabet
of vowels, the vireo's dialect,
Genesis in a bush.
The first paragraph of summer
spelled and respelled
in the syntax of the sparrow,
in the finch's uncomplicated grammar
until summer ends.

Only the beginning of fall translates
in the bare prose of the crow
in the apple orchard,
while the small birds are silent,
and the hawk circles in and out
of the undulating afternoon.

This I Heard in Winter Mountains

This I heard in winter mountains
from owls in rime-spangled trees:
break off a slip of old witch hazel,
dowse deep streams that never freeze.

Dowse deep streams beneath the ground
that flow the way the planet turns
and fill deep caves with lightless pools
never crowned by trilliums or ferns.

This I heard in winter mountains
from hawk and fat snow hare,
from blackbirds in the cat-tails,
and otter in a snare:

dowse deep streams that always flow,
never choked by stones or snow,
never arched by boughs or bridges,
never ruffled by swimming boy.

In the Beginning

In the beginning was the breath
before there was the word:
the bright vowel of birth,
the dark vowel of death.

After the breath there was the word,
in the long hour of the dream,
untroubled and intricate,
beset with peaceful beast and bird.

Before the flesh was made,
there came the ghost,
a faceless figure in human shape
casting no shade.

Midsummer Past

for Dorothy Wordsworth

At nightfall we sat in the orchard
and talked beneath the apple trees,
listened to the owl in the cedar
and to our voices lost in the leaves,
thought of the fruit unripened,
weighing down the loaded boughs,
heard thunder in the mountains,
felt the warmth rising from the ground,
understood the labor of the root,
undoing layers of rock,
felt the strength of darkness,
prying open the bones of the earth.

Doves

Twelve snow-white doves
maneuver all morning,
in perfect formation
in the windless summer air

over rooftop and steeple,
pine tree and fir,
hill and lake town,
while a hungry hawk,

on a nearby branch,
follows their every move
with icy agate eyes,
and, targeting the smallest,

dives on swift humming wings,
steel talons grappling
the hapless dove.

A snow white feather,
and one red with blood
sail away on the wind.

Sea and Sky

*The sea and the sky remain the same.**

The eye discerns a shape upon the beach,
far out upon the headland, half in fog
and half in light, the shape of man or woman,
wearing a dusky cape and a peaked hat,
suspended in the half-light, the sea's and the land's,
among the broken stones, a hunter, slave
or fisherman shivering with cold.

The ear hears a voice coming from a stone,
a woman's or a child's crooning in dark undertones,
the sea's voice or the moaning wind's,
voice answering voice, sea answering sea,
memory listening with the ears of all the dead.
On hands and knees upon the sand, the ghost
gathers pebbles and shells to mark the time that's left

before ghost after ghost must turn and join
the restless dead deep in the groves of spruce
whose branches and snake-like roots
coil and coil around the moss-invaded beams
of ancient houses turning them into punk and dust
beside the burial posts raised to hold the dead
beneath sky and sun, rain and wind.

Where great poles lean carved with bird,
and beast and fish, artful raven, lord of everything,
great whale and sovereign eagle, wings beating
to fly off into eternity, beak shrieking into the wind,

let ghost dance with ghost in a wheeling ring
around the golden spruce whose light
has turned the earth and sky into gold,
tree upon tree, beach upon beach,
star upon burning star.

* Anthony Carter, *This is Haida*, Indian Heritage Series (Vancouver,
  B.C.: Agency Press, Ltd., 1968), p. 100. This poem was written after
  visiting abandoned Haida villages in the Queen Charlotte Islands,
  British Columbia, in the 1980s.

Taymuusya, Rock Wren

What news do you bring, little Chatterbox,
bringer of news? What's the latest
gossip on the hill?
Who is playing around
with whom?
Whose fledglings have an unknown father?

You sing the same thing over and over
all morning on a sage branch,
over the broken stones,
until I am sick of hearing it.
The same old tune and worn-out words.

I am not a liar or an alarmist,
but I did see the dark shadow of a
hunting hawk, circling the cloudless sky.

Furthermore — under this branch,
on the broken rocks, a rattlesnake,
the biggest I have ever seen
lies as still as a stone,
its cold eyes opened wide,
its tongue flickering in and out.

What did you hear?
The dry sound of rattling on the rocks,
a sound beyond sound,
it chilled me to the bones.

Then nothing. No more sound,
not even beyond sound.
Beyond stillness.
Only the imperceptible hiss
of the rising wind
as the snake slithered off.

The rock wren is a bird of the shrub-steppe of eastern Washington
State. *Taymuusya* means "news bearer" in the language of the Yakamas.
See Jack Nisbet, *Singing Grass, Burning Sage: Discovering Washington's
Shrub-Steppe*, A Nature Conservancy of Washington Book (Graphic
Arts Center Publishing), p. 99.

Credo for a Simple Life

You ask me if the owl recognizes its next of kin,
if a seed knows its father
or the mole its mother.

How should I know?
How can I know what I've never dreamed?

I lead a simple life,
have simple tastes,
spit out resinous seeds,
drink wine that is turning sour, gnaw stones instead of bread.

But I have not forgotten the ground,
have never renounced the air
or damned the rain.
The dark and I are not enemies.
I recognize something of myself in everything.

The raven's wing feathers provide me with a roof.
The deer's hoof prints point my way home.

From Green to Gold

What was it that you said? The swathed light fell
across the green peninsula. The rocks
lay this side of darkness, lichen-laid
among the constellated mosses. Mist
rose from the alder-circled marshes.
And the great blue heron, stilted in lilies,
knew leaf from frog. The heavy morning breathed.

What was it that you cried? The bending sky
broken with rain beyond the edge of light
was a blue weight upon your hair and shoulders;
your wrists were wrapped in leafy shadows barred
with light. The nervous spider, furred and angry,
arched in a corner of the web you broke
when you stepped toward me by the stone-choked water.

What was it that you meant? Flames burst
around you and you stood in white-hot light:
snakes coiled around your ankles, and you laughed.
Your face became a place of rocks and thorns.
Heat and thirst beyond endurance,
your eyes as blank as a desert,
the shadow of your hand
fell like the shadow of a scorpion across the stone.

Go Hawk-Watched

Go hawk-watched from the yellow cliffs
above the waterless arroyos and boiling swamps
through wilderness acres of salt and fire,
thorn-quick among the blazing bushes:
hot noon of stillness on the brown plateau.

Go dry-tongued through the scarlet afternoon
across the lava steppes,
snakes looped around sage and rabbit bush,
the jackal always at your ankle.

Into twilight go, across the border
toward caves and trees, and take the grassy pathway
up the mountain side in an ascent of breaths.
Go with a stitch in your side and aching thighs,
moonrise unfolding twisting valleys below.

Finally, you will sleep.
No bells in granite towers will chime the hours,
or quail cry by the wells.
Let this be your own country,
these meteor-pocked hills,
these rocks consigned to flames.

Scene

The end of the year burns away.
Bonfires banner the hill.
Tamaracks tumble into yellow dust.
A meadow matches the sea.
Fence posts measure the length of the wind.

Between the estuary and stars,
the sky teems with wings.
Otters slide down muddy banks,
deer leap over pointed grasses,
pigeons discover a rooftop.

Maple leaves collapse into ash.
The ash will abide and not the tree,
though the wind shall shoot it across the sky —
abide with the lake's dark legends
and the hills' long story.

October

Something in your face and hair remind me
of October's fields, its yellow moon,
its aspen-quaking streams.
The merest wind buries me in leaf-fall,
among the tall grasses brushing the stars.
Wild geese speed high in arrows pointed south,
escaping certain snow.
Owls are all eyes among the firs,
and ice chains the pond to the ground.

Winter

Love has lost its luster.
The rose will not bloom again this year,
its roots, now thwarted and shriveled by the first hard
frost, only to be released in April by the first caress of
spring after long sleep and silence
and broad widths of dark,
while the white moon sails away
light as a feather over the frozen grass.

Idol

Leap from the rock into the darkness
among the bleached bones and the withered flowers,
while the emerald idol sits dreaming, eyes fixed on its navel.
Mimosa perfumes the air where the catbird calls.
Should night pass away and the wild starlight,
the nameless galaxies, the drunken stars and wobbling suns,
and all the gods and goddesses turn into hollow faces,
what shall the flame consume springing from the metal
                                        glimmer?
The stroke of flint against the edge of granite?
Often enough the ghost shall beat in vain
on the marble door of his tomb
when the mimosa is gone and its perfume vanished
and the catbirds are birds of bone,
and the idol and the rock and the darkness are one.

Stilleben

A perfect apple, two plump plums and a paring knife
arranged upon a table, a blue vase of yellow dahlias
and asters, a half-filled glass of purple wine,
a green-striped tablecloth askew, a corner bunched in folds,
an open window giving out on the level sea,
blank, but for the banking wings of a single gull,
create an image of uneasy peace.
Solid objects ready to spin out of the frame
rearrange themselves into lines and planes,
with a minimum of color, only shades of white on white.
Better yet an empty canvas,
the world as it appears in the back of the mind,
shadeless, weightless, vacant as it really is.

Madam

(Vienna, 1952)

Fabelhaft is the word she used
over *Milchkaffee* and two croissants.
Morning lounges in her lap with two chihuahuas.
In an hour the sun will be at its zenith in her hair.
Girls, pretty as geraniums, giggle in the valleys of her chin.
Sexilingual she speaks all those languages and more and
        the language of love.
(Sex is a word she never uses.)
Her son is the president of a firm —
Allgemeine Gesellschaft something or other
exporting shoes to Africa.
"*Er ist ein* nice gentleman."

Every year the geography of her body
grows more turbulent.
Scandinavia is stamped on her forehead.
Her ears listen to Romanian wind.
Her lips taste the Pyrenees.
Her feet dance in the Sahara.
Her breasts are huge with all of Asia.

"It's not what I wanted, to be sure.
Je viens d'une bonne famille, vous savez. Très Catholique, très propre..."
She is an Alp. Her ore is pore.
Her girls are all *sehr elegant.*
"Even the Archduke, the one at Sarajevo, I mean . . .
Yes, war is terrible.
Die Atombombe . . .
Ich meine doch . . ."

Rocks

I read rocks, volume after volume
of granite and basalt,
in a library crammed with stones stamped
with fossil print.
I flip over page after page of slate,
I scribble my name on a sandstone wall,
fumble in dust, gasp for air.
My bones are scattered on a stony shelf.
My skull grins at me from a half-dark niche.
My fingers study their bones.
Spine and shoulder blade have a lot to say.
I wintered here before the flood,
knew Noah before he built the Ark
and sailed off into the dark
with all the animals of air and water.
In library stacks, stone piled on stone,
shelf after shelf,
I choke on clouds of antediluvian dust
laid down, grain upon grain, in a world without time.

Harass the Crow

Harass the crow,
the beetle and the snail
with frost and hail,
with freezing rain and snow.

But spare September's fruit,
the grape and spear of rye.
Let calm winds sweep the sky,
cool water find the root.

But the crow will die in the glade,
and beetle and snail upon the ground.
The light will change and slowly fade,
the last leaf fall without a sound.

Tundra

The winter wears a color all its own,
a colder place to hold the soul alone.
Black lichen covers blacker stone.
The winter wears a color all its own,

a colder place than soul has ever known,
deep in the tundra at the edge of bone.
Winter is colder than the cold alone,
the coldest place the soul will ever own.

Deeper than the deepest fossil bone,
winter sinks into a darkness all its own.
Far off in the tundra at the edge of stone,
absolute zero eats away the bone.

The World They Die In

The world they lie in is the only one.
The summer follows them wherever they sleep,
surrounded by the richer flora and
rarer fauna of the world they keep
around them in the cool light of the moon.
The shadow of the heron falls across the sand:
the crying of the water birds is distant and deep.

A star's cool light will shine on them
and glimmer on the river stones.
The salamander will flee from them,
darting into darkness at the path's near edge,
slipping through the water's roots, its leaves and stems.
The light's bright anger and the water's wrath
pour down upon the dying in their age.

The world they sleep in is the only one,
filling their ears with sounds of wild birds singing,
abandoning them to momentary light.
The intervals of shadow in a leafy glade
between the moon's arrival and a comet's fall
in the long and gold oracular night,
leaving them dreaming in the world they made.

Early Autumn

In early autumn the river flows warm and shallow.
The sea-wind barely stirs the leaves.
I walk behind my restless shadow
as it crosses the border between waking and dream.
Is this the peace that morning promised?
The soothing calm that noontime brings,
relief of laughter in late evening
among the yellow southern houses?
Now waking is half of dreaming in a night that does not end.

The sky, abrupt above the willows,
trembles as a thousand wings
wheel across it, flock after flock of weary birds,
home at last in the thick bushes of the south.
Where is the tree of wisdom
that you grew from a doubting seed?
Autumn grows more ominous
with the thunder of a vacant afternoon.
Pigeons fly off the roofs of empty porches,
widgeons whistle over the rushes.

At the crossroads, a man and woman stand together, head
                                               to head,
their words blown away by the wind.
The first act of their drama was a promise of something to
                                               come.
The second ends with a problem to be solved,
the third with death and burial on a hill.
The morning arrives with the sound of bronze-tongued bells.
The play has ended. Another begins.
The moon has set and darkness waits.

The Gates of Autumn

The gates of autumn all fly open.
The crows patrol the pasture as if it were their own.
The wind no longer curls itself asleep around the trees.
Wasps suck the nectar from the rotting fruit,
pears and roses mingle their scents in the air.
The lake has turned into a shining glass.
Swans dip their black bills into the water.
I think of Hölderlin walking home from France,
his mind wandering on a different plane.
I imagine him locked in his room,
explaining through the open window to a friend
how wind increases half way through the night,
shaking the pear tree, sending heavy fruit
thudding to the ground, tearing the roses from their stems,
scattering broken blossoms across the lawn,
rattling the weathervanes on every rooftop.
The storms of autumn wait for the year to end.

Her Winter

Winter deceived her with summer's weather;
the golden light of leaves and wings
beneath a flawless sky she thought she saw.
She dreamt of water and watery things
in a richer region nearer than the snow,
a southern province an archipelago
of perfect roses and gullies of quince.

And woke, blaming her age
for aching bones and wrinkled skin,
fingers groping for a stick,
eyes straining to see beyond the windowpane.
What had that crow cried on the river?
"The eye sees what it wants to see. A crow
is still a crow in summer or in winter."

But still she dreams of southern suns.
What good are clothes upon her skin
if they let old bones freeze,
though she gets down upon her knees
and prays for weather she danced naked in?

Light Lingers

Bonfire light lingers on the last leaves of the year
still clinging to the boughs

reluctant to let go and fall
to be swept up by the wind
into the waiting flames.

Darkness takes the leaves that still are left.
A storm takes the lowering clouds.
Lightning ravages the pears still dangling
from the boughs.
The storm will take what is left.

A wasp's nest in the eaves breaks loose and falls.
What stays is nothing but a dying star
too far from earth to concern us at all.
Only a whisper from a friend's dead lips
can tell us which way to go.

The Tree of Life

The golden tree of Life,
the pale marble tree of Death
grow side by side on the gold-flecked bank
of the river dividing life from death,
their branches so entwined they cannot be told apart.
The golden tree crowned with gleaming foliage and fruit:
sweet-scented leaves, pomegranates, figs,
and bough after bough of gold-skinned pears,
spilling onto the ground from the overloaded boughs.
The pale tree's branches, black and distorted,
clawing the tattered clouds.
The gold tree's towering trunk and bountiful boughs,
forged of the purest ore from the virgin veins
at the earth's deepest core.

Textbooks

Before the U.S. era of Vietnam is finished,
the episode will have provided many chapters
for future American history textbooks.
— Rich Gotcher, newspaper columnist

First, read the tears of Asia
on millions of cheeks
and then translate them into prose
that can easily be read.

Who will index them
in our histories?
Who will proofread
the blood of a child?

A dark wind shakes
our industrious continent
and rips away the smoke
from the stacks of our mills.

Will there be enough paper
for all that should be said,
mountainsides of newsprint
stamped with destruction,
phalanx after phalanx
in Roman type,
charging our eyes,
assaulting our ears?

In an ink-black winter,
an animal moans:
pity whelps a pitiful litter
in a thicket of print.

Chronicle

First there was the flood that broke through the dikes
and freed the river, vomiting slime and mud
over the drowned city for a month
of drenched cats, floating buildings, uprooted trees,
banks littered with sodden books, a horn and a lute,
maggoty cattle rotting in the bushes,
where the branches had caught them,
a raven and a crow sharing the head
of a drowned pup.
And then came fire, a holocaust of flame
started by a boy lighting candles for the dead.
A hound bitch had whelped on the porch of a floating shack.

What water had not claimed, fire devoured:
images of kings and saints in stone.
A scripture of smoke and flame unscrolled
across the sky for the living to read.

Finally the looters broke through the border,
poured through the battered city gate.
Chalice and icon decorated the quilted tent.
Fire hungered for what the flood had spared.
Summer lightning struck the general's statue,
melting bronze in mineral flames.

The Lion of Kabul

Pity the lion on his couch of dung and thorns,
pity him his eyes lost to a hand grenade.
Pity him his silken coat, crawling with lice,
raw with mange.
Share with him his diet of ashes and pain.
Praise him for his strength in the face of dread,
King of the Pride, Lord of the Plain,
broken King through no fault of his own.
Drive away the boys tormenting him with sticks and stones.
Shield your eyes from the dazzling light of his crown.

In December 2001, television news reported on animals remaining
in a small zoo in bomb-ravaged Kabul. Among the animals was a gaunt
male lion blinded by a hand grenade, and fed by a lone zookeeper
with scraps the keeper found in the rubble of the devastated city. This
poem was begun in the first week of January 2002, and finished on
January 26, 2002, the day the lion died.

Season in Hell

Abyssinia grew for him
    hot flowers in the sand.
A black bird flew out of the desert
      and ate bread from his hand.

Tonight, prowling jackals scour the plain
    under desperate skies.
In a tangle of bush and thorn,
    a strange bird cries.

Eurydice in New York

How cold her limbs, her bloodless skin!
She descends the slanting labyrinth
down folds of granite, lips of lime,
her ankles woven to the thongs of pain.

How black the gulf, the edgeless gloom,
the ledge along the river of the dead
where shadows bend from no light sprung.
She shivers with cold and dread.

Outside, the street lamps smolder in the rain.
Tires hiss along the asphalt lanes.
She stumbles on the roots, cutting her feet on stones,
not daring to look at Orpheus at her heels.

On, on she winds the river darkness down
slowly among the loosened stones,
and hears the river break upon the shore,
the long boat knocking on the rocks.

How far the mourning music of her lover's lyre.
O glance that lost her to her death again.
For all her story and earthly glory:
the spiral ivy and crimson berries of the yew.

I Hold a Beast, an Angel, and a Madman in Me

I

Hail to the angel in your skin,
the haloed figure of your body's trance,
wearing your light and singing with your tongue,
its eyes the eyes of your devouring glance,
the kneeling image of a holy play,
singing the music that the lute has sung,
recalling what the pattern of the fall had been
and what dark Lucifer had sung that day.

II

What of the beast that howled across your dreams,
the werewolf prowling through the desert of your pain,
the shape half-human with the hollow eyes,
hounding your heels and whimpering at your thighs?
What of the beast that gnashed your omened palms,
that grappled at your wrists and stalked your brain
across the plains of dying, green with tombs?
O chain him to the rock above the dust of Cain!

III

Grope for no mercies of the madman you,
the spectre thin as fog within your brain,
the sinuous lust erect against the dark.
O listen to his ravings blue as doom.
Swiftly the dry stones drink the raging rain,
and thirsty for the moon the damp dogs bark.
Morning will come as mournful as the curlew.
Your hands have felt the structure of your tomb.

The Dust of Stars

The dust of stars rains down on earth
and settles on the man who sleeps too deep.
A light can't help him where he goes.
Somnambulist exploring dangerous planets
his dreams invent: cliffs and chasms to give
him nightmare sweats: voracious animals
pursuing him in endless tangled forests.
What ominous star rules over his fear?

Some filthy animal's long hair had brushed
against him in the dark. A hideous hag
with naked dugs, misshapen, blue with cold,
her lidless eyes following his travels,
had stopped him on the path beside the stones
beside a well deeper than he cared to know.
A ravenous rain devoured the earth,
houses and towers and uprooted trees.

He summoned superhuman courage
to look her way into her gaze.
Drenched to the bones in freezing rain,
he turned and fled along the slippery stones,
and slipped and fell and screamed,
awakening to wonder what her eyes
had meant to say to him in love or hate
that left him so afraid and old.

Say Death

Say death dies with him in the freezing room,
a dying man at the end of his breath.
Death for him was never a certitude,
only an inconceivable event
to be scoffed at by the callow young.
So he lived with no plan or purpose,
savoring only the excitement of a risky hour,
for him there were no haunted places,
no dark birds fleeing fire or a falling tower.

In Old Age

What love now needs is a home,
not just a habitation,
but a place to be oneself,
a place to be alone with one's thoughts,
room for a bed, a cup, a book,
space for a breathing, warm-skinned body on a frame of bone.

Yet what love needs, it cannot always have:
a good bed and a wooden table spread
with the whitest cloth, set with blue china plate,
with milk and coffee, marmalade and bread.

But what love really needs is time to know
what it has always known, like
a Latin verb *amas* and *amo*,
learned by heart and not forgot —
or the name of a plant or an herb:

rosemary, sage, and especially thyme
crushed by a heel among crowded stones:
relentless creeper,
homonym of time,
savor and savior of broth
distilled from meager bones.

Confiteor

Bless me, Father,
for I have sinned,
mocking the water,
cursing the wind.

Bled into birth,
born blind and red,
I spat on the earth,
laughed at the dead.

My bones' tall shadow
and the shadow of my flesh
danced to the shallow
whisper of ash:

enacted a passion
to the singing flame,
actor of inaction
on the stage of dream:

wearing lewd vesture,
ample of girth:
of diffident stature,
unnerved by mirth.

Walking with a swagger
though slightly lame,
Christ the Tiger
stalking Christ the Lamb.

Driven by derision
into the hands of pain,
having buried decision
in the dark of the brain,

and played a minor part
upon a shallow stage,
devouring my own heart
and vomiting my rage,

I, bone and marrow,
flesh and blood and ghost,
body and its shadow,
howl in the falling frost.

For the Gods

I have ground grain for the gods,
laid out salt and bread,
gathered the sweetest black grapes, the juiciest purple plums.
Tongue-tied, I stammer out the names of the gods.
Father of fat, mother of bone,
save me from fire and whirlpool,
death by flame or drowning in swirling water.
Grant me the peace my horoscope promised.
Orion finds the thrush at nightfall in the elms
as darkness overwhelms both bird and song.

The Wise Men

One winter wise men, white as ice,
traveled from paradise to birth
led by a planet red as blood
above a redder earth.

Following the flame in a cloud
they passed a lake that, like a glass,
mirrored their shapes and shades.
Bleak stone gave way to grass.

That week it snowed. Their fingers froze.
Two moons wheeled with the earth.
The wise men reached the border
dividing paradise from birth.

They found the boy in a dung-caked crib
guarded by shapes half-human, half beast,
who squatted on the sodden straw.
A rustle of wings rose in the East
and seven shining angels sang
outside the door. This story women tell,
who blue with cold, walked barefoot
across the snow from paradise to hell.

Sleep

I take my sleep from a tree or a stone,
a snakeskin or a feather wafted away by the wind.
What I need is someone to take me in,
a flowering branch nailed to a wall
as a welcome sign.

I take my dreaming
from the body of a dove,
light-boned, soft-winged,
born of light and love.

Prophets

Out of our passion in the last black hour,
we pick the everlasting flowers that bloom at noon.
Out of our lunacy under a motionless moon,
in a place where neither wall nor tower
mark the valley or point to the hill,
we search for the mothers of David and Saul,
and for the daughters of Solomon who call
out of the darkness and the air that has grown so still,
as if time were to stop and an angel fall.

The Chisel

He carves his own death.
Behind his forehead, there glows
the marble dream of tombs.
His mind's coiled vision
unwinds at his chisel's blade.
Heraldic in his Duke's lost dream,
death awakens to haunt the shadowed face
under a helmet bannered with snakes.

Death melts from stone.
The thinking hand warms to the chisel's haft.
Hammer and iron tooth
unshield the bone,
unmask the worm.

The Golden Plain

Beyond the forest
there shines a golden plain,
littered with ruins and gems,
glittering in the sun.

Close to the ruins
the sea breaks in,
diamond bracelets
around its arms.

And beside the sea
amidst the ruins,
a woman leans
against a broken column,
among white timeless ruins,
waiting for me.

Enough of Dancing

Enough of dancing and the dance:
the dance will end as it began,
arms and thighs, heels and toes
timed to the beat of insistent drums.

The love you learned from constant dreaming
is still the love that once you spurned.

Think of the famous art of Yeats,
the craft and cunning of the poet.

Thought dies along the burdened nerve:
passion unlocks the gates of love,
but nerve and flesh are not your own,
and bone is all that's left of shapely hands.

Bring on the dancers! Begin the dance
beneath the burning summer stars.
The dance will end as it began,
the dancers in a whirling trance.

Clown

Allow me one dark hour with the owl.
Let rain fall, fire break out, thunder, wind, and hail.
Roll back the black night noisy with wings,
blotting out the stars, brushing away the moon.
A Barbie doll belts out a ballad in ancient Greek,
a puppet dances, dangling from a string,
a dog prays in an unknown tongue.

Let me still breathe at midnight through my teeth.
Frost and fire will consume the moon.
The Furies will arrive and all of the Muses,
to sing and dance upon the sand.

The mask you are wearing is nothing but brass.
It can never turn into gold in all eternity.

Remembering César Vallejo

The light will not hold
    but slips into darkness again
    between two black stones,

will not hold over the sea face,
    the inlet, the lip of land,
    the eel grass and thick black mud,

will not hold but will slip
    into darkness again along
    the brief lifeline of your palm,

will slip into darkness again
    in your black pupils,
    two black stones.

An earlier version of this poem appeared in *Rip Current*. It was revised in May 2002.

The Witness Tree

If in the span of a hawk's heartbeat I could cast a spell
upon this blank white page lying before me,
and transform it into acres of ground sprouting grass and
trees sending their roots into the ground,
until an untamed forest fills the page for miles and miles,
from corner to corner, edge to edge, crowding the margins,
strong trunk soaring with trunk into the windless air
from horizon to horizon fading into dusky blue,
ridge after ridge to where the sea begins,

> in the clearings we are able to gather armloads of lupines in the
> shade of limber pines,
> before straying from faint pathways in the amber light,
> to stumble upon a witness tree and get our bearings again,
> Section 20 Township 22 Range 16 E,
> a morsel of claret mountains,
> a slice of surveyed valley,
> a microcosm of America,

we could believe that ages ago a chisel of depthless ice
had carved a trough across this land,
had inched inch by inch for a thousand years across this page.

Scarred granite scalped the earth and scattered
what was left of the mountains across the page,
preparing it for the roots of a poem.

Rome: The House of Keats

It's too late to drown off Leghorn
or cough to death in Rome:
be Shelley, white and sea-torn,
or Keats upon a cot.

The image still
grows from the sorrow.
The death mask stares
from the wall.

Flower sways by flower
on the stairs to the Trinity:
Father and Son
and Holy Ghost.

The Maker is
the Breaker.
And all those crones
hawking flowers on the steps
can only assure you
that he has
a steady hand
and takes what he gives.

Paul Klee's Hands

Watch Paul Klee's hands.
Keep your eyes on them
as they move purposely
across the blank white page,
the chasm, the eternal void;
watch his hands like the ends of cedar boughs,
dispensing cones and seeds
across the bare ground.

The Poet Dances through his Poems

Lithe Harlequin of somersaulting images,
he dances through his poems, leaps through hoops
of words and walks upon his clever hands,
smart clown whose pantomime makes children laugh and clap
their candy hands and taunt him with balloons
and sticks as if he were a painted cat,
an animal comedian playing man.

In his trim garden left partly wild,
this tidy plot of trees and flowers,
of glades inhabited by all the beasts
and birds, mythical and real, he dances on
to croaking toads and trilling birds,
to children humming and dancing, dancing and humming.

Le Système Nerveux

Le plus grand poète, c'est le système nerveux.
                              — Paul Valéry

The greatest poet is the nervous system as Paul Valéry
                              once said,
poetry being the result of an interaction of nerves.
The act of writing is like driving down a dark road
at midnight, not knowing where we are,
tuned to the signals of danger, blinded for a moment by
                              approaching headlights,
reflexes take over, a crash is averted,
nerves are on edge all the way home.

There are things more important than all this fiddle-faddle
    as Marianne Moore said.

In the dark of winter
we dream of the light of summer.
Les abeilles d'or swarming in the orchard
in the breathless blue of early June,
the new queen on her nuptial flight,
supported more by light than air,
the drones pursuing her, the lucky drone mounting her
                              in mid-air.
Then, his luck gone, he explodes into nothingness . . .

And so at the epilogue of summer, the spider's elegant web
anchored to the glassless window frame
billows back and forth but does not break in the wind.
A harrow rusts in a dusty corner of the vacant barn.
We endure the end and beginning of another life.
Gold is scooped out of absolute dark.

Poetry

Poetry, that whore who lewdly sings
her bawdy songs into the poet's ear,
turns breasts into mountains, wombs
into caves, and makes paradises of desire
of gardens of common flowers

wounds and woos him,
the fool, tantalizing him with visions of her naked body,
bores him with her posturing,
coos over him, soothes him, tortures him again and again,

scorns him, quarrels with him, weeps for him,
reduces him to a spaniel-tongued man.

Whore of midnight fornications,
mockingly she sings to him,
naked in his bed,
and he is ready again to die in her arms.

from

Now, a Thousand Years from Now

(1975)

—

Roots

for Olive

I try to remember where I have been.
A dead snake loved this dust.
A she-hawk hovered over that nest.
The sun crashed down behind that hill.

I heard the wind's harps
in the same trees,
scraped through similar weeds
over different stones.

Thunder shook the mountain tops.
Old grandfather of our dead tribe,
how he barked!

Like a flint knife slitting a deer hide,
lightning slashed the sky.

In the fossil darkness
among my mother's bones,
listening to the lapping voices
of her blood
in her fern-branching veins,

rocked in her roots,
I crouch between the pathway
and the human heart.

Indian Song

I was born on a river
with a slow voice
in a country
of lichen and rock.

The bird-tracked hand
of a woman
laid me on the ground
on the top of a hill.

I watched the lynx,
listened to the locust,
waited for the hawk
to talk to me,

while the sun howled
in his yellow skin
and the wind sniffed my shadow
on the hill.

The Fleece of the Ram

Mei: *Beautiful: a big sheep. Abbreviation*
for Ya-mei-li-cha, *America.*

I / THE ROOT*

1

Suppose the key word to be "antipode" . . .
the river grips the virgin rock.
   The person who contracted to build my boat
   engaged to have it in readiness by the 20th inst. . . .
      set out at 4 o'clock p.m.
      under a gentle breeze . . .
      a succession of grasses, trees,
      marshes teeming with birds . . .
      current strong with riffles,
      oars hard to use.
   A dove flew safely through clashing rocks.
   The kingfisher hovered over white water,
   scolding us, many small birds
as thick as insects, twittering in sedge.

And this medesene man could foretell things . . .
that he had told of our coming into their country,
   and they thought us gods dropped among them:
   helmsman, navigator, peacemaker of tribes . . .
these natives have the Stranges language . . .
but I found them much pleased at the Dancing of our men,
the women passionate, fond of caressing . . .

* The spelling is that of the Lewis and Clark journals.

she was so beautiful that when she slipped into the tent,
the storyteller could not tell his story . . .
dancing, giving away hir bracelets . . .
   the old squaw, half-blind, crouching in a corner
   had lived more than a 100 winters,
   & when she spoke great attention paid to what she said.
The roots of the rock outlive the crown.
   And "my boy Pomp" had his monument.

    2

One set of Gold Scales
       to weigh the industry of tribes,
       their language, traditions, monuments,
       the extent and limits of their possessions . . .
           Is suicide common among them?
I have done the business. My good Servant, give me some water.
He had shot himself in the head with one pistol
& a little below the breast with the other.
       The wind grapples open grasses, rocks, trees . . .

The unknown scenes in which you were engaged . . .
       the promise of a city
       at the confluence of rivers . . .
       or a place near Sea and River
       resembling the situation of Alexandria
       with respect to the Nile . . .
a root they have, efficacious remedy in cases of the bite of the
                       Rattlesnake.

       To these I have added the horns of an animal
       called by the natives the Mountain Ram . . .
       Under his hair he is clothed with a very long fur,
          shines golden
             in the sun.

II / BETWEEN 1827 AND 1927

1

The moon pulls great waters.
How articulate the wind is in the leaves,
but it does not want to tell me who I am.
I think I am somewhere between sleep and a stone.
I ask the sun where I have been.
My father, mowing grass, does not know.
My mother does not want to say.
I taste weeds to understand what a bird sings.
I am an Indian all day
under the plum tree in the backyard.
An old blanket pinned to grape laths
is my tepee. I am Chief Bear Skin,
last of the Yakimas to smell free wind.
The wind cannot tell the distance
between 1827 and 1927,
nor can I.

2

A photograph, inked too black, in the newspaper,
of three Yakimas, a brave and two squaws,
wears the same scowl. Pennsylvania Avenue in 1901,
stumps down the middle, watch-fobbed Saxons in front of
                                                the hotel,
was what my mother saw.

You look like an Indian! You look like an Indian!
My mother's black Italian hair,
tossed over her forehead, dries in the sun
on the back porch.

       Ka-e-mox-nith was so beautiful
that when she stepped into the tent
the old men stopped talking. When she left,
their voices were like the dry scraping of insects
in the yellow pines.

     3

Old and sick, Wah Kukhiah rode up the Yakima Valley
with his daughter to the forest.
At the foot of the mountains
he told her to go home and rode on alone.
In the half-darkness at the edge of a scree,
in a dazzle of light, a stranger sat
on a boulder, looking at him:
"Do not be afraid. Close your eyes,
and you will see."

     4

The plum tree in the sunlight
sways in the last warm wind,
branch dancing with branch.
With a bow bent from a willow switch,
I shoot an arrow straight across the garden
into a bed of hollyhocks.

I got him! My tribe will not go hungry.
I know who I am!

III / MAY 1927

My forehead bows to the sound of water,
       faint through trees.
A warbler in the lilac answers
       a warbler in the pine.
May spills over, fluent with leaves,
       redundant in the mirror of the pond.
Happy in weeds, I dawdle through trout lilies,
       gold on the hillside,
       nibbled over by cows and butterflies.

       Stooping over corollas,
       I own their nuggeted anthers,
       and break stem after stem
       to bleed against my palm.

Wild with the incense of cottonwoods,
by the hobo dump, wreathed with early smoke,
the river curls, ice in the town's arms,
sleepy with salesmen and women,
haggled out of dreams,
money under every pillow,
under every hill,
wise with the intercourse
of vaginal mines.
       In the schoolroom's chalked silence,
       I perspire, stranger to the fists
       scrawling virgin paper with accusing consonants.

IV / THE CEMETERY

Love your mother's face
bowed over blossoms,
her hands arranging them
for your grandfather's grave.

In the front yard,
two bushes of lilacs,
tall as the house,
one white and one violet,
bloom every year
for Memorial Day . . .
       Walt Whitman dead for thirty-seven years,
       the Civil War over for sixty-four,
       the olive-backed thrush or the hermit
       singing in the canyons around the town.
Your grandfather, for whom
Victor Emmanuel meant more than Lincoln,
wrote from the Shoshone to his dying mother in Italy:
Don't despair of Death.
E una Gran Bella Cosa.

"You'll never make Americans
of these goddamn wops,"
the foreman said.

In the cemetery,
a Mediterranean bay of blossoms,
white and violet in coffee-can urns,
billows against the stones.

V / THE COAL MINE

Somewhere deep in every American heart lies a rebellion
against the old parenthood of Europe.
    —D.H. Lawrence, *Studies in Classic American Literature*

Don't bullshit me, Mr. Lawrence!
How shall we recognize our own fathers
       in caos converso,
their palms bleeding in the fossil damp
while the Johnny Bull boss roars at the end
of the tunnel in the Eocene dark,
and the carbidian flames in the middle of their foreheads
pitch pantomimes of shadows
on the ultimate wall?
How shall we tell the flesh from the shade it throws?
Tu credi che qui sia il Duca d'Atene?

VI / THE RAM

In sheep-grass weather, clear bells found me.
I climbed to hear them while I slept.
Sheep grazed the hill above our house.
I heard them nibbling in my sleep.
Jangling bushes tossed on my pillow.
The walls baaed with the browsing flock,
yapped with the fox-tailed dogs. I ran toward
morning, blue above my father's gate.

A dry breeze rattled the dusty pines.
Pack horses, nudging luminous grasses,
flicked their tails after flies. My ears followed
the oaths of Spanish herders.
I raced the hill slope after the easy flock,
slipped, quick as a lizard, under barbed wire,
whipped across an acre through a cloud
of pollen, gold upon my arms;

waded through briars, tangling my hips.
A thistle snapped at my thigh. I cleared
a meadow, over the mine of a mole,
past a lark, warbling to weeds.
A pigeon tilted equal wings
against the light I made. Wide-awake,
I leaped over the dreaming flock and sank
my fists into the fleece of the ram.

The Coal Mine (1931)

1

There are many ways to sleep.

When I was ten, I slept
deep enough for roots,
far enough for a wind
from infinity to find me.
The wind's time was mine.
The cricket repeated at nightfall
what the katydid rasped
all afternoon on the pile of ties
by the railway siding.

I played under the arc light,
climbed home to the moon.
My mother's hair illuminated her bed.
My father's walk was dark and long
down the incline to the bituminous seams.

In the tangled underbrush,
the thrush sang and sang.

2

The next day,
the mole's domes
redeemed the yellow pines
from the heat at the headwaters
of the Yakima River,
defined what counts —
the coolness of roots.

3

Where I am, I dream.
A wind from the peaks
curls up in the hollyhocks.
The energy of a whole afternoon,
gathered in one trumpet flower,
bells back a fanfare to the sun.
The late light hangs, a hive from a branch.
A leaf is what the sky needs.
A spider strings a wire from rose to rose,
lies in ambush
like a lion at the edge of a veldt.
One father's as good as another —
earth's or Eden's —
watching the spider
pounce through light.

I cannot see the light.

4

I wait for the man-trip.
The dark takes me down.
My father kneels in the deepest mine.
I rummage through other tunnels,
explore wider entries
humming with different hoists.
Fossil leaves flicker across my palms.
I dig into old earth
above older rocks.

I hear buried streams
filling with silt.

5

Black is the color of my father's hands.
Black is for death.
My father is more than that.
I can see in the dark.

6

My veins carry my blood away
into the same dark
past his roots.

He Never Wished for War

In winter my father spoke American.
In summer Italian was for the leaves.
For him, grapevines looped over every backyard fence.
Leaf mold was always ready to take him
where he cared. Love was where the roots were.
He never wished for war.

When goldenrods powdered the roadsides,
and balsam roots multiplied the sun,
his thumb favored the apple,
tested the ripening plum.

He sold the Chev and planted pear trees
on the driveway. In time, fruit
bent the boughs. On winter evenings,
slicing D'Anjous with his penknife, he feasted,
licked ambrosia from his dripping thumbs.

Homecoming

By memorized ranches, houses named by heart,
barbed-wire fences wound the dreaming miles.
Colts nuzzle mares in tooth-sheared pastures;
red barns, like hens, squat glad in dust.
Tires grind to a stop in gravel. Frogs declaim
American from ditches creamed with spawn.

Wind flaunts the scarecrow's sleeve, who grins
away the garden, gloating over dandelions.
The sow snores in her dream of milk and corn.
Licked by a momentary sun, straws blaze
upon the gateside muck. Calves bawl.
Light drowns the honeysuckle on the wall.

The Graves of the Indian Women

1

Welling up out of invisible crevices among the boulders,
secret holy places only your ghosts visit,
the dark seeps like your death blood across the ground.

The blind moon, oldest crone of your tribe,
sinks on her knees, groping for your bones
scattered by grave robbers in the dying summer grass,
her fingers fluttering from grassblade to grassblade
with the wind.

     Oh, you were beautiful!
     We pity your dead bodies.
     We pity the chiefs and braves who loved you.
     Their hands are leaves that will fly with the fall winds.

     Their mouths are mountain flowers in the high meadows,
     bent and broken by early snow.
     In the low valleys, mullein and heal-all
     smoulder to cinder in their arms.
     They wade knee-deep in your dust
     and in their own.

     Another summer corrodes Major Garnett's iron wrists
     and the wrists of his men who set fire to your tents
     and chased you and your children barefoot down the
                          valley
     after they had cinched five of your braves to pine trees
     and crumpled them, five shots splintering the
                           crystalline air,
     leaving them for coyotes and crows . . .

Your ghosts drift away now with your chiefs and braves
and the stars and the full summer moon
down the white gorge of eternity
with deer and elk, grizzly bears
and mountain goats running before you forever
over loose stones and gray roots.

2

But you always return
to haunt our own broken stones and dying roots.
In the late fall, if we listen closely,
we can hear your ghost voices under the cottonwoods.

One of your sorrels, long dead,
neighs by the stream edge.

3

This morning, we finished stacking firewood
on the cabin porch against the mountain winter.
Two jays bickered all afternoon
in the sunlight in the bull pines.
The lake no longer reflects geese speeding south.
The mountains are weighed down with darkness.

4

It is midnight.
The fire is almost out.
The cabin's one room is cold, and we blow out the candles.
Wrapped in our blankets not far from your bones,
we shiver at the first breath of snow from the east.

A cougar
     padding across pine needles beside the door
     barely ripples our first sleep.

     In our dreams tonight, and yours, behind walls
     and walls of snow piled upon snow,
     now, a thousand years from now,
     the cougar pads across the dying coals.

The Beaver Dam

L'espèce des castors serait très préférable.
— Voltaire, *Dictionnaire philosophique*

The day after the president was shot,
my son and I climbed to the beaver dam
beyond the hill crest in a logged-off hollow

unkempt with slash and muddy water, and sloshed along
the wheel-scarred road, gashed through a hemlock grove,
fertile with toadstools, nurtured by hard rains,

Amanitas, sinister, perverse
with many deaths erupting through the musty humus,
until we reached the pond's dark bulwarked water

where clever sluices lapped an ancient stillness,
snared by the snags between the squalid clouds
and littered earth. We marveled at the dam

and lodge the beavers had built, the alder trunks
chiseled into stout logs, chinked with mud,
a watery farm for a contented family,

the dozing kits snuggling against the walls
of their domed house, and marveled at that life,
old as a fossil, like a diorama

of a glacial age, anachronistic
upon a complicated and human earth.
Nootka whalebones clouted slaves to death.

The lynched half-breed kicked Okanogan wind.
The *Tonquin* reddened green abundant harbors
with beaver blood. But chisel teeth cut clean,

the father's and the son's, by crystal ponds,
although the steel-jawed rushes still betrayed
them for the coinage stacked upon their pelts,

and stockade guns marched slaughter to their domes,
the tomahawk and blunt square-headed axes,
black jewels in the mud. . . . Turning, we thrashed

our way through devil's club and iron briars
back to the bull-dozed road above the town,
its roofs already echoing with funeral drums.

From the Top of Quartz Mountain on the Twenty-Fifth Anniversary of Kandinsky's Death

From the top of Quartz Mountain:
deer, trees, the shapes of stones
— hexagonal crystal, blemished agate —
the great perfection or an imperfect emblem
from the deepest heart,
the tips of the elk's great antlers brushing the aspen leaves.

The light blows strong,
remembering to sing:
thalassa! thalassa!
over the black wave,
through the forked branch of the pine,
> (At Neuilly, Kandinsky,
> precise as a chemist,
> mixes his own colors,
> lifts the shade at one o'clock sharp,
> letting in the light.
> Between the necropolis and the Champs-Elysées
> the rainbow arches over the iron gate.
> In the center of each painting,
> zero is absolute at the bone.)

On the top of Quartz Mountain
the sun shifts from spruce to pine,
and the late afternoon shadows
dapple the deer at the edge of the scree,
the golden plover in the grass by the western hemlocks —

> when suddenly the sun explodes,
> black begetting black at the edge of red.

> Yama, how your blackness shines,
> a black bird in a nest of stars!

Grizzly

The webbed toes of waterbirds padding
estuary mud kept me awake for hours last night,
although wild geese, lost in fog,
lifted me almost to the edge of dream:
unclouded larches, pure Canadian fords,
peaks that contrived to blend their colors
with the tatters of a dying sun.

Meanwhile, my heart-beat timed me
back to a sleepless earth,
but toward morning I climbed a high moraine
against a wind from the North
and slid down into a Yukon of faultless woods
where I hunted the Grizzly in a foot of snow
and tracked him down into a bog.
Waist-deep in water, I flailed my arms.
A flock of widgeons whistled over my head.
The sweet smell of the beast hung in my hair
and penetrated my skin through my dripping clothes.

> Furred, my hands stretched their claws
> and scratched at the early stars.
> I felt a blizzard blowing under my hide.
> Sleepily, I dragged myself to a pile of roots.

> In a nest of leaves
> I slept that winter out.

The Blind Poet

A poet gone blind dreams he sees
the winter moon float out of the alders
and sail over field after field of snow.

All summer long, light leaping off stone
was light lost upon his face:
early June's, as cool as evening rain;
the light of mid-August, tangled in goldenrods,
burning more burnished than his figurative sun.

October spilled not light but smoke
of smouldering leaves across his sleeve;
he tasted ashes, stumbled through dust,
swallowed his own kind of fear.
A later light tightened around his face,
a golden mask on a frame of bone.

Now he sits motionless
beside a window glassed
with northern nights, frosted by his breath,
watching the moon sail over
the lost snow fields of his mind:
pure light, pure metaphor.

Branches

Near Lugano or at Borgeby Gård
(What does it matter if snow
obliterates a vineyard
or bends birch trees to the ground?)
Rilke, head bowed at his desk by the window,
ignores the falling snow.
The poem he is writing
grows like a squiggly black vine or tree
on a snow-blinding page,
vine shoot, pliant birch branch,
trembling on an infinite wind.

> Zero catapults through his brain.
> He hunts out a metaphor in space.
> Frost grapples old roots:
> branches crackle in icy air.

> At home in the Okanagan, snow
> piles up for days against the cabin walls.
> Coyotes circle the winter camp.
> A bull elk starves to death in the streambed,
> walled in by a dozen feet of snow.

At this last moment, let essential ice
grip our heart wood-vine, birch,
pine tree in western mountains.
On their knees on ancient stones,
the gods feed branch after branch,
> twig after twig-pine,
> birch, vine shoot
> into original flames.

> The ashes of our poems
> drift away on an infinite wind.

from
Rip Current
(1986)

Rip Current

un passage pour l'Egypte se paie en or . . .
— Arthur Rimbaud: an excerpt from a letter he wrote
   from Genoa to his family, November 17, 1878,
   five years after he had abandoned poetry.

I

Out of sea maw
    a frigid wind
    of hurricane force
    late Columbus Day afternoon
    screeches like a fish-eagle
    zooming down for the kill,
    crashes against shore rocks,
    careens into cedars
    spends itself at last
    against vacant mountains
    where its broken wings
    set timber humming
    like a cosmic harp:

(. . . a rip current is a killer
flowing out to sea perpendicular to the shore . . .
suddenly the swimmer discovers he is being swept out
into deep water, waves crashing over his head
almost out of the surf zone,
he goes down and drowns . . .)
    a dark wind ploughs the fallow ocean
    into flowerless clods, grassless humps,
    heaved over the salt prairie, finned
    with sharks nosing out of the depths,
    death snouts in perpetual motion,
    trailing the black raft from the Medusa,

buoyant though freighted with bodies:
can timber be weighed with any more death?

"wafted by stronger breath
by faith and devotion
and meditation realizing the self
freed from the wheel of change
escaping another birth,
forever absolved from sorrow and death."
A passage to Egypt is paid in gold . . .

2

Madame stands too straight in the meadow;
her fingers, tightened around her parasol, bleed.
The dust of willows, shaken down by a bird's wing,
still drifts with the river, and remembers . . .

How she hugged every penny, yet spared no expense
to stage the funeral. Stiff-necked upon a parish chair,
is she counting the pennies traded for the tapers
in twenty orphans' hands or weighing the silver
melting on the choir's eight tongues,
the gold pouring from the throats of the five principal singers?

Think what she must have spent eight years later
to have his bones exhumed and re-coffined
beneath a white marble monument!
Il durera longtemps, if nothing extraordinary happens.

The brass plate on his coffin still gleams like new,
the grave-diggers astonished everything so well preserved —
the box only blackened a little
by its contact with the earth.

One must be cruel, November to May.
A butterfly hovers over a bank of flowers.
All summer long, haze hangs in those trees
or roves the damp grass like a ghost.
      "Yesterday, a day of great emotion –
      at Mass, I caught a glimpse of a young man
      resting his cane against a pillar
      same age, same build, one leg missing . . ."

If a boy gets drunk, it's on the water of the Meuse . . .

      3

In Abyssinia, the desert is quilled
with trillions of blossoms after the rain.
Time is eternal on the threshold of every tent.
The desert is inhabited by wandering tribes.
There are mountains and a succession of plateaux.
Scrub brush and mimosa swarm with elephants,
all manners of ferocious beasts.

      For the leopards, I would use steel traps
      like those we set for wolves at home.

      From the Kingdom of Shoa, I am sending you
      a caravan of gold, musk, and ivory.
      They call me the terror of dogs.
            "Will you tell us your secret?
            Your pen's magic . . . Orpheus' lyre . . ."
            Forced to speak their gibberish,
            to eat their filthy food, to endure
            a thousand annoyances resulting
            from their laziness . . .

one yearns for beeswax and honey,
the pollen of absent flowers
weighing the thighs of bees . . .

all we can do is count on "the tranquil meditation
of daily ritual, the rhythm of sistrum and drum,
of chanting and singing at the great festivals,
rising to a pounding climax in the night;
hidden from the world for centuries,
unknown to all but a few. . ."

Yesterday I gave my burnous to a ragged native,
rode home bareheaded in the scorching sun . . .
Yet, I have never bought or sold slaves:

Les marchandises que nous importons
sont des fusils (vieux fusils à piston
reformés depuis 40 ans),
. . . 7 ou 8 francs la pièce
60,000 cartouches Remington à 60 dollars
le mille . . .

But don't take me for a capitalist:
all my capital at present amounts
to 13,000 francs
and will be about 17,000 at the end
of the year.
Late a teacher of French and languages . . .
recently deserted from the 45th Regiment of the French
Army. . .
Shit on poetry! Don't mention the word to me!

"I am ill at the death of your brother.
I feel as if my soul has left me."
Ras Makonnen

4

Dear Sister,
All I want to know is how are things at home.
Are the crops in?
Have you picked the apples in the orchard?
How much did you get for the grain?
Are the cows still giving milk?
How should one translate:
*"Ne ruissellent-ils pas de tendresses et de
lait?"*
"Do not stream by fire and milk?"

Send me the best French translation of the Koran.
And buy me a theodolite, barometer, rope, and telescope . . .
and send me the following books:

> *Le parfait Serrurier,*
> *Manuel du Verrier,*
> *Manuel du Fabricant de bougies,*
> *etc.*

although there are no locks on the doors,
no glass in the windows.
The beeswax candles burn slowly and softly
at evening in the tents . . .

I yearn for the chalky desert of . . .

5

. . . mon existence périclite . . .
I leave everything to the mountains
and to the rivers.
Only the trees are honest,
and the stones.

Tell me when I am to be transported abroad.
                    (A rip current is an insidious ocean action
                    that can exhaust the strongest swimmer.
                    Fortunately, the swimmer can tell
                    when he is in one.)

                    Persistent, the bloodstream courses
                            secret channels,
                    replenishing, heartbeat after heartbeat,
                            a sea without end.
                    Spirochetes, like sharks, cruise
                    after rafts laden with the shipwrecked,
                            the living and the dead,
                    at the edge of reefs
                            beyond unattainable atolls,
zig-zags and terraces which would take an infinite time
                    to ascend . . .

Monday morning, they are amputating my leg.
Danger de mort. Affaires sérieuses à régler.
            Take the fastest train!
            L'insomnie perpétuelle . . .
                    not eternal sleep.

For the night, an injection of morphine.
The Abyssinian harp burns in my hands.
My speech, the results of years speaking another tongue,
Oriental or African turns of speech,
or merely morphine or delirium,
do not discount memory and imagination . . .
            I say the strangest things, very softly . . .
            a continual dream . . .

         better to be damned in eternity.

J'aimais la mer . . . comme si elle dût m laver [me laver de ces

                    abérrations] souillures . . .
                    *Salut à la bont . . . ***

We call for help. No one hears over the surf's roar.
Panic takes over, then exhaustion.

        Count us all among the drowned.

* From the rough draft of Rimbaud's *Une Saison en Enfer.*

Photographs with and without Sound

Tomorrow we shall be able to look into the heart of our fellow-man, be everywhere and yet be alone . . .
— Laszlo Moholy-Nagy

1

Edward Weston
I am not asleep
just resting my eyes
and marking time
ein Augenblick,
leave me be
you wait so long
for the right moment
to capture what you see
and do not see

2

March weather is
hit and miss
sunlight splatters down
with snow and rain

the creek draining the draw
meanders and dawdles
under matted salal
and huckleberry bush

the wind scours barnboards
until they are off-white,
sweeps away old dust
creeps away with a broken spine
to whine under bent grass

frugal *Hausfrau*
the blackbird whistles
bending a hemlock spire
so easily another inch

that is the way the eye operates
recording what is old in February
and new in March,
this year last year the year before

not even the sharpest lens can catch that
one blackbird whistles to another
downstream
a million years ago

3

We see what we do not want to see:
the invisible made visible
on an April day:
hear and do not hear a small song
in the leafless twigs,
believe and do not believe in the reality
of a white-crowned sparrow
in its scrubby home,
head thrown back in dissonant song —
a sewing-machine-whirr —
preceded by four plaintive notes,
enthralling us as we watch and listen,
showered with dew.

A sickle moon
is nothing but a shadow
mowing insubstantial stalks of light.
The real moon roves out of sight.
A real bird sings a note we cannot hear

until spooked by a dark wind
it darts away.
We backtrack into silence along a winding path.

For a moment the hygiene of the audible,
the health of the visible
slowly filter through.

On this Side of the Mountains
Where You Have Never Been

I remember you otherwise, not so far from home,
your mouth not a black stone,
your hair not a nest of spiders
in this damp orchard invaded by alders,
on this side of the mountains where you have never been.

Once in Rome three days before Christmas,
a long time ago, farther from home than you had ever been,
leaning out of the window of a scrubby hotel
on the Piazza di Trevi, you believed the stones
while the opulent fountain dashed cold water on your face.
Two silver coins gleamed on the table
to pay for your passage home.

In the broken bowl of the Coliseum
spilling a cobalt sky out of one end,
you met a woman in a purple cape
who read your fortune in the palm of the arena,
your too brief lifeline drawn in sand and stones.
You gave her a lira for her ticket home.

Now on this orchard floor, patterns of light and shade
come and go and are always the same.
Do our mothers straddling our graves
bring us to birth a second time?

I see you walking where you never walked before,
toward home through the drifting leaves
still smudged with gold, happy, whistling,
your hands in your penniless pockets.

Tarascon

I want to believe
that the wind from the river
roiling the beds of lavender
in the station yard
will lash out with the same fury
tomorrow and tomorrow

that the woman who sails over
the grimy station floor
on glass feet
her ankle-length gown
molded to the bones and muscles
of her black body
will glide over the floor
tomorrow and tomorrow

now that the snows have melted
in the pastures around Lanslebourg
from the rooftops of Briançon
the wolves no longer slink down
into Paris during the coldest winters

the moon sifts and sifts
the dust of dead poets
from palm to palm

Grave at Sète

for Paul Valéry

Beyond the last American ridge, on the cliff edge,
      blue burns to gold at the zenith.
We shade our eyes, glad for eagles;
      count them with one voice.

Before the future year,
      we hold on to their holy circles;

      start from zero:

         the grave under the pines,
         the thud of a falling cone sending
         a tremor through the Italianate tomb —
         the frozen eons of spheres.

The wasp halting at the entrance of her nest
is hammered into gold by the sun.

Sesto Calende / Lake Maggiore

for Eugenio Montale

I press my face against the train window
hoping to catch a glimpse of the red turtle doves
flocking into Sesto Calende for the first time in anyone's
                                                memory,

while the young doctor, the blue ox yoke he bought in Milan
spanning the luggage rack above his head,
chatters on and on with his two daughters, one dark, one fair.
    The ox yoke will adorn their mantel, he says:
    sky-arch over earth-fire.
    Everything comes to pass.
The mountains at the border melt into each other.
River water melts into lake.

We enter the tunnel under the numb alp,
finally rejoice in Swiss air
between blue wind and gold.
    The fire blinds us all.

In the Mine

Every morning, the ten southern windows of my father's house
reproduce ten copies of the sun.
They blaze like ten sunflowers all morning
in the blue plate glass
while my father kneeling in the deepest mine
orders the dark to curl into a ball
that he will place in a corner until he is ready to do
what he had not dared to do before.

Ten minutes before noon, the glass begins to buckle
with the energy of so much light battering its skin.
Balancing the ball of dark upon his palm,
my father holds it to his ear, listens to it hum
fossil music, clear as the voice of extinct leaves
singing on a long-dead tropic wind.

When grosbeaks and waxwings settle on the limbs
of incandescent firs ten seconds before noon,
the ten windows shatter, scattering blue splinters onto the
                                    ground.
In the mine my father hurls the ball against a wall,
stoops to gather the pieces and fit them together again.

The Dead Poet's Worktable

Ornery old mule browsing the linoleum's starved grass,
your sway-back free at last of your pack
stuffed with papers and books,
your scarred legs spared the switchbacks, the slippery riprap,
the long climbs around the screes,
your master's curses and his hissing whip
no longer bullying you
around each perilous bend;
you will never negotiate another trail
in the full summer heat, buzzing with hornets and flies.
Do you still dream of peaks sparkling in sunlight,
still sniff the clear cold air above the timberline,
yearn for a deep drink of icy water after the sweaty haul?

It's been a while since the dead poet,
that cantankerous mule driver,
turned you out to pasture forever.

Beads

I'll not take back what once I gave: the dark kiss
from my golden mask's silver lips,
but will take back again what you will never miss —
the crimson garment that clung so tightly to your hips,

and leave you the frame on which it hung,
clean and empty but very beautiful,
like a useless string on which red beads were strung
by fingers that were especially careful

not to spill them on the floor
to be gathered by sons and daughters on their knees
and be locked unstrung in a box for

ever and ever and ever. Imagine a hive of bees
surviving all winter on honey the color of the sun
until the combs are sipped clean, one by one.

Lessons

I learn to sleep from a stone.
Waking, I learn from the branches
in a bright wood.

Mornings, I go to school with the mole,
and study all afternoon with the beaver.
The hawk teaches me how to soar.
The crow lectures me in the simplest prose.

But my words are not for keeps.
Who I am is not mine to save.
The ant is less ignorant than I.
The sparrow knows more than I do.
His song has no end.

I envy the wisdom of the spider,
the knowledge of the rose.

At night, in my dreams, I practice
what I learned all day.

The Tower of Silence

I

We lay our dead, naked, on the tops of towers
to be picked clean by the birds,
gliding in on the wind, reptilian,
hawk-beaked, harpy-winged,
ripping out heart and lungs,
sea and sand, as one, blazing in the sun.

A procession, blue on the seaside,
led by a hag in a cowl,
circles the cape at the seamark.
Gulls and their shadows haunt the stones.
The horizon blurs in a haze of silver and white.
The wind answers the bird-voiced bones.

The doors in the tower are all shut tight.

II

He came from a death's distance away
through more intense silence than he had ever known.
Not even Procris, lying on the shore
surrounded by herons and indifferent dogs
created more silence in the way she lay.

And then he summoned music from the strings,
plucked a wilder lyre than he had on earth,
strummed song out of chaos,
a beginning of form
growing out of the light that followed him
to where she stood among the rocks
faltering toward his song.

All the nightingales of Greece,
made wild, sang in the serpentine dark.

O the dead are young forever and ever.

III

The earth is his poem: the sun, his metaphor.
Fire sings like a bird on the stone.

Having broken the sacred circle, murdered
the she-snake coupling with her male
at the marsh edge among the yellow mallows,
a goddess' anger upon him,
he was turned from man into woman,
fluent in the language of birds,
the kingfisher's, the crow's, the heron's,
the jargon of the wren.

IV

The laurel tree is for change —
        but only into death.
He wrapped his arms around its trunk
in front of the grotto
        by the beached sand,

an old man, ivy-wreathed,
drunk, wearing a tattered dress,
a string of bells jangling around his waist,
        blind, shrieking in falsetto,
        frightening the doves
        in the sacred trees,
        so they flew away and back again,
happy *Grossmutter,*
muttering incantations to the wind.

Lady of Dark Places,
          take him by the hand,
          guide him over the rocks
          and around the slippery logs
          at the river mouth.
Do not let him fall.
Open a pathway before him.

          V

A branch in the hand is an eye,
the seasoned wood of cornel,
a staff in the hand of the blind
to see the way along the sea path,
the rocky road to the ships,
the beaked ships of the warriors.

A bird for the blind is a voice
that speaks the country's language,
the measured words of wisdom,
the level call of truth
on the dusty sea path
by the beaked ships of the warriors.

The sun on the sea is a flame,
kindling the charred sails
and broken oars of an autumn voyage,
propped against the splintering keels
of the beaked ships of the warriors.

from
Dog Star
(1990)

Time

Time, the mongrel bitch,
limps along on three legs
up and down both sides of the street,
sniffing each bush and clump of grass,
every garbage can overflowing
with a whole week's waste.

She holds a bleeding forepaw
tightly against her chest
and whimpers from time to time.

Not long ago on a greasy pallet
in a basement,
she whelped a dozen pups
sired by Pity, a hopeless hound,
toothless and blind.

Piebald and wall-eyed,
all of them have succumbed
to accident or disease.

In heat again, trailed
by a troop of panting mutts,
she is ready for another round
of births and deaths.

Lilacs

The lilacs are in full bloom
in every corner of the overgrown yard.
I smell them everywhere.
The spaces between their blossoms and leaves
are blue caves, swirling with dust.
Roofs and cupolas of a foreign city
seem to float out of the haze.

But in the nursing home next door,
the air conditioner announces the first warning:
by autumn the necropolis will be full.
There will be no more room for the living,
not to speak of the dead, in the mausoleum.

But there will still be time for love
after so many loveless nights,
a time to get drunk on wine
after so many months of thirst.

Marston-Bigot, Somerset

New Year's Eve, 1945.
1262 Engineers Combat Battalion,
billeted on the grounds of the former
country house of the Earls of Cork.

Some crazy bastard from Company A
sets off a couple of real road busters
precisely at midnight on New Year's Eve
in the orchard below the chapel and manor house
of the ninth Earl of Cork,
blasting the old year out, the new year in,
frightening off the owls from apple tree, pear, and plum,
rocking the earls in their graves in the churchyard,
setting the tower bells jangling a ghostly change,
rattling the German glass window in its frame.

Somewhere a wall falls, and another,
and a last year's hornet's nest
drops from the eaves to the ground.

The stage properties belonging
to the Admiral Company — 1570 —
overflow the world's bins:
there is no more room in the world
for all the world's junk:

1 rock, 1 cage, 1 tomb, 1 Hell mouth;
1 tomb of Dido;
1 glove, & 1 golden scepter;
and the city of Rome . . .
1 golden fleece; the cloth of the Sun & the Moon;
2 coffins; 1 dragon in Faustus;
1 wheel & frame in the Siege of London;
1 crown with the sun . . .

A long ways off, a long time ago,
Mole shuffles across the carpet in threadbare slippers,

proposes a toast, as soon as Rat and Badger are seated,
        to the fire on the hearth,
          the fire in their hearts.

Morels

In mid-May
among the first trilliums,
under the pines and white firs,
the first morels,
feigning fir cones,
push up through humus and duff.

We fill a basket,
sauté a panful in butter,
smack our lips over the taste of earth.

Kontrapunkt

I crave another body.
This one will never do.
I have had enough of these arms.
I envy a bird's wings.

I no longer want these fingers.
I crave another body.
This one will never do.
I think of the river's hands
shifting pebbles from palm to palm.

I cannot see the wind nor hear the light.
I crave another body.
This one will never do.
The goshawk's eyes
can always locate the right wind
to soar in: her ears can hear the light
speeding past her.

I crave another body.
This one will never do.

Shades of Gray near Brussels

Black laid beside white
dissolves into gray.

"I am writing you
from this backwater in the hills
straddled with barbed wire . . . "

A rooster and six blue geese
practice close order drill in a red brick courtyard.

A man with a scythe
slashes at a bed of red poppies.

Blood-red petals litter the walkway,
plaster themselves to our heels.

The figs of Carthage are plumper than Rome's.
The senators get the message,
rub new salt into old wounds.

We shall never be rich.
No use hoping for prosperity.

Still, there is no money in being patient . . .

The Orchard

Dear Sister,
Our brother is here with me and has built me a house,
Russian-style, of wood, on the property I have bought
for my riding school. How strange, yet how appropriate,
it looks under the evergreens of western North America!
      — Letter from Colonel Nikolay Petrovich, a refugee
        from the Russian Revolution, written forty-five
        years before his death and the sale of his riding
        school to land developers.

We no longer love or hate, gloat over victory,
despair over defeat. The bare winter cherry trees
still gasp for ampler light in the darkening orchard
beyond the white board house your brother resurrected,
nail by nail, from his Russian memories into American reality.

Beside the front stoop, cotoneaster berries, ablaze,
consume the concrete steps and wooden rails,
reducing them to ash. Upon the stable roof
a copper pony, blackened by year-long rains, jogs
along an iron arrow shot east by the wind. We no longer
weep or smile, dare look boredom in the eye,
though you forgave the wind for sending the holly bush
tumbling into crimson dust at Christmastime,
while the pheasants fed by your lady's hand,
plump and clucking, scurried off into the brush,
and your collie, quailed by your bandaged death,
sniffed a corner of the garden swept clean
by autumn of grass clippings, weeds, and life.

Now, beyond the hemlocks and weeping cedars,
we imagine a black curtain slowly falling
at the end of the final act; hear whining saws,
trees crashing to the ground.

Fragment from the Vienna Woods

In the orchard the snails are multiplying
under the dead leaves and wet grass . . .
The pasture gates all fly open.
The shadows of poplars crisscross the lawn.
Slate roofs glimmer across the quiet lake.

The sun gets down on its knees,
strikes steel against flint
sending sparks flying into the grass,
tinder too damp for flames.

The wind meanders all afternoon,
unable to make up its mind which direction is best,
east or west or both directions at once.

Moles own all the stones
and the mounds of dirt planted like domes across the lot.
The poet's black thrush calls all day in the black wood.
The poet dies by his own hand.

At Mödling, near Vienna, where Beethoven
wrote his *Missa Solemnis,* the pears
are rotting on the boughs.
Golden nuggets turn brown in the sunlight and shade.
Kein Eingang! Keep Out! No Admittance! — not even to
                                        Ludwig,
strolling there, hands clasped behind his back,
the *Gloria* echoing in his stone-deaf ears.
Arrested as a vagrant, all he can do is protest.

Rain falls hopelessly on the foreign spruce trees.
We picnic by the side of the road.
"Grüss Gott," a man, wheeling a bicycle by on the roadside, calls.

"Grüss Gott to you too!
Grüss Gott to everyone!"* we call back.

Possibly from the Gaelic

At my right hand: a grassblade.
At my left: a lily stem.

On my right: a dry, white, withered tree.
On my left: a black thorn bush.

At my right hand: a red-topped mountain.
At my left: the face of a blue plain.

On my right a ruby is a dying ember.
On my left a diamond is a splinter of ice.

A white mare limps away with the world in her belly.

I Cannot Teach You

I cannot teach you how to write a poem.
I have a hard time writing one myself.

They say Paul Klee had peculiar eyes
that could see into and beyond
a person or thing.
But he could not teach anyone to draw.

I have heard a row of poplar trees
fades into nothingness
before the north gate of Turin.
Someone saw Gottfried Benn there
sitting at a table in a dark café.
What a hand! What an eye!
Read his poems on love and death.
But he could not teach anyone
how to write a poem.

The wind keeps blowing in and out.
No one, not even itself,
can know its mind.

Love . . .

Love requires you
to cut off your right hand,
to dig out your left eye
and bury it in the gravel pit
safe from dogs,
to limp along on one leg
and a black stick,
to despise your neighbor
and hate your face,
to chew pebbles and spit out glass.

But deaf and dumb, blind and lame,
ignorant and foul,
I would still love you,
body and soul.

The Night a Chunk of the Moon . . .

How could we forget
the night a chunk of the moon
plunked into the lake,
sending tons of water splashing
over hawkweed and dandelions,
and thousands of starlings splattering
like dust after an explosion
into the air?

The stones cried out in pain
on the roadbed.
They couldn't move.
Blind milestones wept for a hundred miles.
One mile was as long as a thousand
for the fleeing ants and snails.
One minute was as long as a century
for the dying butterflies.

What light was left in the chunk
that fell that night from the moon
drained away into the lower valley
flooding it to the brim
with the palest light
we had ever seen.

Limitations

1

An old man — he looked a hundred —
with his long dirty white beard,
Walt Whitman whom I had
never heard of, the open-collared poet
smiling, seated in the back of the omnibus
bumping over the cobblestones —
there he was now, sitting cross-legged on a trunk
and grinning at me
in the back of the side-show tent, its flap up,
in that dingy carnival while out in front
in the brilliant booth: Come on, kid,
get your hand off your pickle.
Spin the wheel for only a nickel.
Take a chance.
How can you lose?

The old man winked at me, and I winked back,
seven years old in new overalls,
until my mother came flying around a corner
of the tent, and grabbing me by the arm
and screaming my name, pulled me away.
That dirty old man! she said.

2

We erect boundaries between heart and heart,
mouth and mouth. Eyes flash only distrust.

Tongue does not trust tongue.
Words cascade stillborn to the ground.

Deer tracks lead past the cabin door,
lead nowhere but into brush or vanish into knotted turf.

Rain slashes the hillside, huckleberry
and deer bush, a sliver of flint

towering like a monolith above the ant:
stonecrop and saxifrage will help the frost

bust boulders into dust, and more dust.
The smoke from burning slash finds our lungs.

We taste fire, spit out ashes
onto the darkening rocks.

Can we really see what we do not want to see:
hear when a bird voice begins to define

a weightless husk of music for our ears,
the bushy limitations where two birds sing?

Salal and salmonberry prosper cradled by a log
carpeted with hemlock seedlings as tiny as moss

in the alder clump at the swamp edge,
at midday under a milk-white sun.

3

The overripe pears have begun to rot
upon the plate on the linen-draped table
before the painter who looks like a peasant
succeeds in duplicating
in oil and pigment
their solidity, their roundness,
and the taste of summer juice
on a farm girl's lips.

The apples long ago collapsed
into dust.

The half-filled wineglass still leans,
wine black as ink, into the shades of time.
Only the light remains, melancholy,
weightless, golden as fleece,
a cupid's plaster head
absorbing some of the light
but more of the darkness instead.

The old man hunches over his easel
in a field and tries to possess the mountain
for the hundredth time, knowing hand and eye
will finally declare victory over its evasive form.
He farts in answer to a passerby
who asks him if he is painting a cloud or a flower.

The wind begins to whistle with its old fervor
around the mountain.
The old man does not notice.
When he has finished,
the painting of the mountain will exchange places
with the painting of fruit.

The summit of the mountain
shakes in the ever-growing wind,
a hurricane now, sweeping away
mountain and fruit, plate and glass
into the void.
Only two blank squares of canvas remain.
The old painter is beside himself with joy.

Knives

Poems should be
like the knives
my dad used to make
out of old crosscut saws
and car springs,
blue-bladed,
honed to razor sharpness
that could shave the hair off his arm.
They would bend but not break,
their handles carved
out of walrus tusk or walnut,
northern, tough,
perfectly balanced,
fitting the palm,
great for skinning rabbits,
slicing meat from the bone
for the hungry belly.

Late Autumn Barometer

The last of October's hail
and the first of November's black rains
batter what's left of my garden,
send sodden beanstalks, still wrapped
around their poles, crashing into the mud,
and toss my dahlias, scorched by frost,
across limp tomato vines and rambling
nasturtium stems, whose flame-lipped flowers
had raced like run-away flames all summer long
across the ground, still littered with their seeds,
prolific for another springtime.

In the dusk, crows caw down by the swamp,
bickering for roosts in the higher branches.
Beneath my hedge, a toad croaks, once, twice,
like a gate swinging on a rusty hinge —
dead iron scraping iron.

And I tremble with an old presentiment.

At Last

At last I am the old survivor
I always wanted to be,
lingering late in my garden,
scraping the ashes from my shoes.
Humpbacked, I walk with a limp.
Half-blind and deaf, I read the lips of the dead.
I can say hello in nine languages
and goodbye in twenty more.
Old friends are used to what I say.
All winter, I have nothing to do
but set hopeless traps for wolves.
My wife knits gloves
for the village children.
Crows come and go
in the cottonwoods by the river.
The hour hand is missing from our clock.
Sometimes the minute hand goes wild,
sweeping time before it
so fast the clock dances on the table.
My wife and I dance with it,
around and around
all night until the sun
spills through the windows
and lifts us off our feet
and carries us away
like a flood.

To the Lady Kung-Sun

Lady, dance out your dance!
Let ankles do what wrists foretold.
The stars of China are so cold.
Dance on, dance on in a trance!

The dawn wind rattles cabbage leaves.
Roosters crow in muddy yards.
Your dance will laugh, though now it grieves.
Dance, dance upon the two-edged swords.

And spin the cobweb of your glance
to ensnare the moths of the night to come.
The stars are flutes, the moon a drum.
The yellow grasses dance when you dance.

The Pathway

The river meanders where mountains cannot go.
I skirt a field where doves take wing.
Overhead, the power wires sing and sing.
Upon the lakeside, the wind breathes slow.

The shadow of a silver snag floats in the lake.
I gulp ice water to slake my thirst.
Three hawks hunt, loose-winged over trees, immersed
in the slack light their circling makes.

I choose a pathway into black trees.
The hawks still drag the light they made.
The wind tracks me down into cold shade
through maidenhair fern and anemones
and grapples at the roots of my hair.
The pathway drops off into empty air.

Le Voyage

O cerveaux enfantins!
— "Le Voyage," Charles Baudelaire

I

For the two boys fascinated by maps
and *The National Geographic*,
oh, the happiness of going somewhere,
the planet shrunken to a ball on yesterday's page,
yet how immense in the pool of light under the lamp!

Getting up in the first light
to a thousand white Leghorn roosters
crowing in everybody's backyard,
to the wailing whistles of the black locomotives
straining uphill to Stampede Tunnel
with a mile-long string of freight cars
clanking behind them,
we shiver in our BVDs, blind fingers
hunting buttons and slipping them home.

We leave, heads wreathed in flames,
ride off to the pumping rhythm of the pistons
of our old black '23 Chev
down the gravel road that winds on forever,
past fenced fields and pastures,
the meadowlark dribbling
flute notes across the dripping grass;
we lift our faces to the wind,
drunk on blue space and light,
the sky blazing overhead;
sail past islands of pine glades
floating in lakes of lupine in bloom,

so much blueness around us,
so much more heaped ahead,
blossoms so dense under the pine trees,
pillars crumbling and falling,
the weight of Venice,
lighter than goosedown,
yet too heavy for its golden roofs,
walls and stalls giving away to the awful tonnage
of so much blue air, the golden horses
charging across the blue lagoon.

II

. . .   heartweed scattered along the roadside,
heart leaf, heart root,
heart scald, heart grief,
heart's-ease for the lovelorn,
heart-whole for lovers,
heart balm for the sleepless,
heart break, heart ache
for what has never been,
for the unseen, the unheard
beyond Lost Lake on the way to Quartz Mountain;
the trail along Fortune Creek
climbing to the watershed
dividing East from West,
dark from light, day from night;
heart wish for the Heart Father,
heart beating in time with heart.

III

Up the valley, a curtain of haze
hugs the mountains' roots, hangs in the hollows.
Mid-morning, the sun will burn it off,
begin to glare in our eyes
forcing us to look at the ground

where the grass is and the stones.
But at three in the morning the air is still cool.
Shadows flank the mountainsides,
lie like pools under the trees.
Love counts what counts:
the distance between light and shade,
the distance between the roadside and bed,
the distance we still have to travel . . .

IV

Bindweed clambers over the roadside rubble,
the detritus of last year and the year before,
binding us to time and weeds.

High over our heads, pine boughs
nurse their secretive blossoms.
        Father Anthers,
        Mother Stigmas,
can you tell us how far we are from home?

We fall asleep beside our father, wakeful at the wheel.
Clouds of pollen shower the old black Chev
in the moonlight under the stars,

        gold piled on gold.

from
A Second Earth
(1997)

—

I Go Back

I go back to my old scars,
wince at the long-buried pain,
taste my wounds on my tongue.

I cry out to you with my uneasy bones,
knitted into an aging frame,
crowned by a hawk-nosed head.

How can I free myself from this shifting light
that turns birds into trees,
trees into birds, rocks into what they are not?

Let the wren burble away in the laburnum.
A blurred animal crouches in a seed.
Expect another birth soon.

Tree

You are all the light you make:
leaf, branch, and bole:
darkness pours from your crown to your roots.
You are perfect and whole

like a stone or a hawk,
a rare kind of gold.
The nights have grown longer.
Day and night are so cold.

What will the young men do
in the light they have left?
The girls will tie on their sashes,
place right foot next to left,

and begin to dance, and dance
through the lightless night.
The young men will dance with them,
place left foot next to right.

More Trees

Hölderlin's Pears

It is not easy to disregard
    the death of trees:
    the long-rooted blossomers
toppled by saw or disease —

great trunk, tender stem,
    leaf and broken bough
    consigned to flames,
laurel, chestnut, hemlock, and haw —

fruit trees, apple and pear,
    loaded boughs that will not break
but only bend, reflected
    in a flawless lake:

the endurance of passion
    that allows the branch to bend
    and not to break
in a day and night that never end.

Campania

Bless the grain.
Bless the black grapes,
the green oil in the jars.

Another winter wheels away with the stars.
Ice gloats that its turn has come again.
Naked trees shiver away their shapes.

Then summer continues its wars,
the brutal sun its raids on the ripening grapes.
Dust lusts for rain.

But summer's loss is autumn's gain.
Rising Venus escapes
the arms of Mars.

Bless autumn's grain.
Bless the bleeding grapes,
the bread on the table, the oil in the jars.

We Count Hours

HAMM: *All that loveliness!*
— Samuel Beckett, *Endgame*

We count hours
from zero to zero:
listen to the termites
digesting the old timbers
of our house.

At sunset, we climb
to the high window over the harbor,
watch the herring fleet sail over the horizon
toward the docks, decks heaped high
with squirming silver
in the light of the rising moon.

The women come out of their houses,
with wine and bread for the famished men.

The Patriots' Flowers

A mè fieul, Màrio, mòrt sël Génévry

On the summit of Génévry
on those wild crags,
on the battle ground
where the fighting raged for ten days,
now that the summer sun
has returned to scorch the stones,
as weightless as feathers,
smooth and colorless as down,
the first Edelweiss flowers
are blooming again.

But this year, if you break off a flower,
you will notice with astonishment
it is tinged
with an already fading half-shade of dark rose
as if a thread of blood,
running from leaf to leaf,
were winding through the plant from deep within.

The currents of morning air
from the woods above
cry out to the pine trees,
rooted on these wild crags
and whitened mounds of stone,
that the patriots' flowers
are the color of blood.

Translated from the Piedmontese of Nino Costa, whose son, Mario, an
Italian partisan, was killed on Mount Génévry in the Alps on August 2,
1944, by the Nazi-Fascists.

Stones

Late August swells to actual green
bestowing reluctant opulence
on common ground. Plain stones
nestling among commingled grasses
beside a mountain lake
are rare jewels. Transported south
and laid among emerald reeds
that bull frogs boom into,
they would be foreign to that place.

Munificence of wilder green,
superfluous with hotter light
would only smudge their luster.
No stone could shine at its best
in air so affluent with reckless vines.

Such stones belong
to higher elevations
beside a mountain lake
like eggs of some antediluvian beast
heaped upon the shore.

I Talk to Stones

I talk to stones beneath deep streams
and ask them what I want to know.

The day is fast, the night is slow.
What dark shades haunt an old man's dreams?

The eagle drives away the crow.
The sun has set; its light still gleams.

Nothing is ever what it seems.
The moon is fast, the stars are slow.

A solar wind begins to blow.
Around, around the sun it screams.

So now, where will an old man go
to find his way, search out new themes?

The ivy climbs, the nettles grow.
What dark destroys, the light redeems.

ABOUT THE AUTHOR

—

Harold James (Jim) Enrico was born in 1921 in Cle Elum, Washington, to Italian-American immigrant parents whose European culture extended to their children. From his parents he learned Piedmontese and Italian, and developed an affinity for languages. From his father he learned to explore the rivers, forests and mountains, and to love the Northwest landscape. Jim entered the University of Washington in 1939 to study music, languages and literature. World War II intervened and he served in the U.S. Army for some four years. He was passionately opposed to war the rest of his life. In 1945, while studying German in New York City, he met Theresa Conroy; they married on St. Patrick's Day 1946. Jim and Theresa had five children and two grandsons.

Receiving his masters degree at the University of Washington after the war, Jim studied poetry with Theodore Roethke and Louise Bogan. In 1950 he studied at the Collegio Borromeo, of the University of Pavia. He earned his doctorate in Comparative Literature from the University of Washington in 1970. Jim taught foreign languages and humanities for thirty-three years in community colleges, including Grays Harbor College in Aberdeen, Washington, from which he retired in 1985. Jim traveled extensively studying poetry and languages wherever he went. Jim began writing poetry when he was fourteen; he continued to write until the last year of his life. His published books include *Now, A Thousand Years from Now* (1975), *Rip Current* (1986), *Dog Star* (1990), and *A Second Earth* (1997). Jim died February 20, 2008.

MARQUIS

Marquis Book Printing Inc.

Québec, Canada
2008